Hello, Family Members,

Learning to read is one of the most important accomplishments of early childhood. **Hello Reader!** books are designed to help children become skilled readers who like to read. Beginning readers learn to read by remembering frequently used words like "the," "is," and "and"; by using phonics skills to decode new words; and by interpreting picture and text clues. These books provide both the stories children enjoy and the structure they need to read fluently and independently. Here are suggestions for helping your child *before*, *during*, and *after* reading:

Before

- Look at the cover and pictures and have your child predict what the story is about.
- Read the story to your child.
- Encourage your child to chime in with familiar words and phrases.
- Echo read with your child by reading a line first and having your child read it after you do.

During

- Have your child think about a word he or she does not recognize right away. Provide hints such as "Let's see if we know the sounds" and "Have we read other words like this one?"
- Encourage your child to use phonics skills to sound out new words.
- Provide the word for your child when more assistance is needed so that he or she does not struggle and the experience of reading with you is a positive one.
- Encourage your child to have fun by reading with a lot of expression . . . like an actor!

After

- Have your child keep lists of interesting and favorite words.
- Encourage your child to read the books over and over again. Have him or her read to brothers, sisters, grandparents, and even teddy bears. Repeated readings develop confidence in young readers.
- Talk about the stories. Ask and answer questions. Share ideas about the funniest and most interesting characters and events in the stories.

I do hope that you and your child enjoy this book.

> —Francie Alexander
> Chief Education Officer,
> Scholastic Education

1

For Ben, *mirus nepos*
— M.B. and G.B.

Special thanks to Paul L. Sieswerda
of the Wildlife Conservation Society
for his expertise

ISBN 0-439-33409-8

Text copyright © 2003 by Melvin and Gilda Berger.

Photography credits:
Cover: John Visser/Bruce Coleman Inc.; page 1: C. Wolcott Henry III/National Geographic Society/Getty Images; page 3: Kim Taylor/Bruce Coleman Inc.; page 4: Terie Rakke/The Image Bank/Getty Images; page 5: Kim Taylor/Bruce Coleman Inc.; page 6: Treat Davidson/Photo Researchers; page 7: Scott Camazine/ Photo Researchers; page 8: Art Wolfe/The Image Bank/Getty Images; page 9: Bradley Simmons/Bruce Coleman Inc.; page 10: Hans Christian Heap/FPG/Getty Images; page 11: PhotoDisc/Getty Images; page 12: Gilbert S. Grant/Photo Researchers; page 13: Len Rue Jr./Photo Researchers; page 14: Dr. Paul A. Zahl/ Photo Researchers; page 15: Norman Owen Tomalin/Bruce Coleman Inc.; page 16: Bruce Clendenning/ Bruce Coleman Inc.; page 17: Steve Cooper/Photo Researchers; page 18 top: Scott Camazine/Photo Researchers; page 18 bottom: E.R. Degginger/Bruce Coleman Inc.; page 19: Scott Camazine/Photo Researchers; page 20: Gary Vestal/The Image Bank/Getty Images; page 21: Peter Ward/Bruce Coleman Inc.; page 22: J.C. Carton/Bruce Coleman Inc.; page 23: Tom McHugh/Photo Researchers; page 24: E.R. Degginger/Bruce Coleman Inc.; page 25: Tom McHugh/Photo Researchers; page 26: Peter B. Kaplan/Photo Researchers; pages 28-29: Anthony Bannister/Photo Researchers; page 30: Steve Cooper/Photo Researchers; page 31: C.K. Lorenz/Photo Researchers; page 32: Art Wolfe/Stone/Getty Images; page 33: Joyce R. Wilson/Photo Researchers; page 34 top: Art Wolfe/Stone/Getty Images; page 34 bottom: Gail Shumway/FPG/Getty Images; page 35:Victor Englebert/Photo Researchers; page 36: Tom Brakefield/Bruce Coleman Inc.; page 37: Gary Bell/FPG/Getty Images; pages 38-39: Ron & Valerie Taylor/Bruce Coleman Inc.; page 40: Stephen Krasemann/Stone/Getty Images.

Library of Congress Cataloging-in-Publication Data

Berger, Melvin.
   Sting! : a book about dangerous animals / by Melvin and Gilda Berger.
      v. cm. — (Hello reader! science — level 3)
     Contents: Bees — Ants — Spiders and scorpions — Snakes and lizards — Frogs and fish.
    ISBN: 0-439-33409-8 (pbk.)
    1. Dangerous animals—Juvenile literature. [1. Dangerous animals.] I. Berger, Gilda.
   II. Title. III. Hello science reader! Level 3.

     QL100 .B48 2003
     591.6′5 — dc21

2002003455

10 9 8 7 6 5 4 3 2 1   03 04 05 06 07

Printed in the U.S.A.
First printing, March 2003

STING!

A Book About Dangerous Animals

by Melvin & Gilda Berger

Hello Reader! Science — Level 3

SCHOLASTIC INC. Cartwheel BOOKS®
New York Toronto London Auckland Sydney
Mexico City New Delhi Hong Kong Buenos Aires

CHAPTER 1
Bees

Most **bees** sting.

You know that.

But do you know why?

Bees sting to protect themselves.

Bees sting animals and people who —

- come too close,

- try to catch them, or

- steal honey from their hives.

To sting, the bee uses its stinger.
The stinger is like a tiny arrow at the end
of its body.
The bee's stinger has
barbs, or hooks,
along its side.

The stinger is
attached to a
special organ
inside the bee.
The organ is called
a **gland**.
This gland makes poison.
The stinger forces, or injects, this poison
into animals or people.
The injected poison is called **venom**
(VEN-uhm).
The animals that inject the venom
are called **venomous** (VEN-uhm-us)
animals.

Every beehive has
special bees
that guard the
honey inside.
These are
called **guard
bees**.
Strangers who
prowl around the
hive better watch out.
The guard bees might attack and sting them.

Bears often reach into hives to get
the honey.
This shakes the hive and warns the bees
of danger.
They swarm out of the hive.
Each bee thrusts its stinger into the bear's
body — and flies away without its stinger.
None of these bees will ever sting again.
These bees soon die.

Meanwhile, the stingers stay
in the bear's skin.
They keep on
pumping venom.
The venom
in the wounds
can be very painful.
It makes the bear run
away—FAST!

Suppose a bee stings you.
The sting hurts.
The venom makes your skin red
and puffy.

Here's what you should do.
- First, scrape the stinger off
  with your fingernail.
  Do not pinch or squeeze it.
  That may push more venom
  into the wound.

- Second, wash your skin
  with soap and water.
  You may hold ice on the spot.
  If you feel weak or dizzy,
  see a doctor right away!

Remember —

- Bees need to sting.
- They sting to protect their hives!

CHAPTER 2
Ants

Most **ants** have stingers.

But they don't have venom glands.

These ants are harmless.

They can't hurt you.

But some ants *are* venomous.

Their stingers are attached to venom glands.

These ants can be dangerous.

One of the most venomous ants is
the **red fire ant**.
It's as small as the nail
on your pinky finger.
Yet it gives a great big sting.

Fire ants live in South America and
the southern part of the United States.
The ants build large dirt mounds.
Some mounds are waist-high.
Hundreds of thousands of fire ants
may live in a single mound.

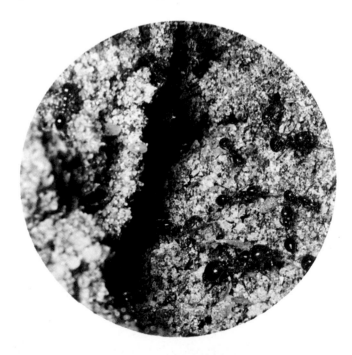

Sometimes a person or animal bumps
into the mound.
This startles the ants.
They swarm out — and they attack.

An attacking fire ant
clamps its jaws
into the
victim's skin.
Then it injects
a dose of venom.
STING!
The venom feels like a poke
with a red-hot needle.

With its jaws locked in place, the fire ant
wiggles its rear end.
It stings again in a different place.
Wiggle and sting,
wiggle and sting,
wiggle and sting.

Soon there's a circle of bright red sting
marks on the victim's skin.

Fire ants have some very large cousins.
Some are as big as your thumb.
They're called **bulldog ants**.
They can be found only in Australia.

Bulldog ants also live in large groups.
Their venom is very strong,
and they attack in huge numbers.
The ants are just like bulldogs.
Once they bite,
they don't let go.

Bulldog ants sting
anyone who
comes too close
to their nest.
Stay far away,
if you can.

CHAPTER 3
Spiders and Scorpions

All spiders have fangs that look
like curved, crooked teeth.
The fangs are long and sharp.
They are hollow on the inside.

All spiders also have venom glands.
Spiders use their fangs and venom
glands to capture their food.

A spider's bite helps make
its food fit to eat.
The fangs force venom
into the insects or
animals they catch.
These insects and
animals are called **prey**.
The venom changes the
solid prey into mush.
And the spider sucks up the liquid.

Spiders mainly kill flies, mosquitoes,
and other insects.

Some spiders eat
frogs, fish, mice,
and other small
animals.
Spiders even eat
each other.
But few spiders
harm humans.

The **black widow spider** is unusual.
It is small, shiny black, and has
a red marking.
The black widow lives in North America.
Look out for it in old houses, garages,
or barns.
The black widow usually hides or flees
when people are around.
But if someone
touches a
black widow,
it may bite.

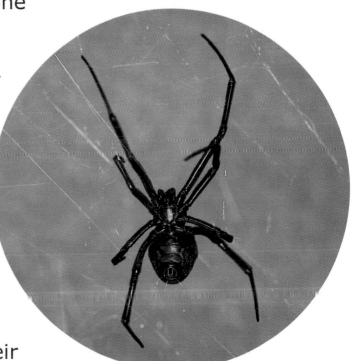

Most
people
don't feel
black widow
bites.
But soon their
muscles begin to hurt.
They feel stiff and are in pain for a few days.

A **tarantula** is another kind of spider.
It lives in warm parts of the world.
The tarantula is large, hairy, and
a little scary.
Some are the size of dinner plates.

Tarantulas eat insects, birds, and mice.
They also bite lizards, snakes, and
wasps that attack them.
But don't worry.
Tarantulas rarely bite people.

A **scorpion** looks like a small lobster.
Here's a surprise though.
Scorpions live on land, not in the sea!

Each scorpion has eight legs
with two large claws up front.
Sticking out of its tail is a stinger.
The stinger shoots out venom.
Scorpions use the stinger to catch their prey.

A scorpion mostly hunts
insects, spiders, frogs,
and mice.
It grabs the prey
with its claws.
Then the scorpion quickly
whips its tail up over its body.
Sticking out is the venomous stinger — ZAP!
The stinger pokes a shot of venom
into the prey.
The prey usually dies.

What happens when a human or
big animal touches a scorpion?
The scorpion lashes out and stings.
The sting hurts.
But it does not usually kill.

Many poisonous scorpions live
in hot, dry deserts.
They seem to like warm, dark places.
One favorite place to hide is inside boots.
No wonder cowboys often sleep
with their boots on!

CHAPTER 4
Snakes and Lizards

Not all **snakes** are venomous.

In fact, only about 20 kinds of snakes

in the United States are venomous.

Venomous snakes have two fangs

in the upper jaw.

The fangs are attached to venom glands.

Some fangs are hollow.

Some are grooved.

A snake's bite pushes venom

into its prey's body.

Most of the time you can't see the
snake's fangs.
The snake keeps them folded back
in its mouth.
Then the snake spots its dinner.
The fangs snap up.
The mouth opens wide.
And the snake lunges forward.

After a snake bites, it often slithers away.

The snake waits for the venom to work.

Soon the prey is dead or dying.

The snake comes back to eat.

It flings open its huge jaws and grabs
the prey.

GULP.

The snake swallows the animal whole —
without chewing!

Can you imagine a snake longer than
a pickup truck?
Well, that's the size of the **king cobra**!
It's about 18 feet long.
The king cobra is the largest venomous
creature in the world!
It lives in Asia.

Sometimes the king cobra bumps
into an elephant.
The snake raises its head high above the
ground — and it strikes.
The cobra chews the venom deep
into the wound.

The elephant staggers.
Then it falls to its knees.
Finally it topples over — dead!
No wonder a king cobra is the only animal
that an elephant fears.

Spitting cobras live in Africa and Asia.
They are also venomous.
But they don't really spit.
They squirt venom out of holes
near the tips of their fangs.
It looks like water shooting out
of a water pistol.
The venom of a spitting cobra is
very powerful.

Spitting cobras usually aim
at shiny objects.
Often these are the eyes of animals
or people.
This blinds their victims.
Then the cobra comes in for the kill.

Venomous snakes once helped win
a battle.
About 2,200 years ago there was
a great general named Hannibal.
He was fighting a battle at sea.
Hannibal had his soldiers collect venomous
snakes and put them into jars.
The men then threw the jars
onto the enemy ships.
The foes gave up without a struggle!

Lizards look a little like chubby snakes with legs.

There are about 3,000 different kinds of lizards.

Only two kinds are venomous.

One is the **Mexican beaded lizard**.

The **Gila** (HEE-luh) **monster** is the other kind.

It lives in the deserts of the southwestern United States.

This lizard does not have fangs.
It has grooves in its lower teeth.
When it bites, venom flows through
these grooves.
After it bites, the Gila monster keeps
on chewing.
This forces even more venom
into the wound.
Gila monsters may chew a victim
for up to ten minutes!

CHAPTER 5
Frogs and Fish

Some animals cannot fight off their enemies.

These animals may be too small.

A poisonous skin helps to keep them safe.

Many **frogs** make poison in their bodies.

The poison oozes out onto their skin.

Animals that eat these frogs get sick.

The poison protects the small, weak frogs from their big, strong enemies.

In one fairy tale, the princess kisses
a frog.
The frog changes into a
handsome prince.
Don't try kissing a frog!
Frogs taste awful.
And the poison will
burn your lips.

Many frogs are brightly
colored.
Those with the brightest colors usually
have the strongest poison.

The colors are a warning.
Enemies that try
to eat these frogs
learn to keep away
from them.
So should you!

Poison dart frogs are small with bright, colorful markings.
They live in tropical forests in Central and South America.

People in the rain forest use the poison from poison dart frogs for hunting.
They heat the frogs over a fire.
The poison drips down from the frogs' skins.
The hunters rub the poison on their darts.
Then they shoot the darts at their prey — and kill them.

Many colorful fish are also venomous.
Among them are the **lionfish**, **stonefish**,
and **scorpion fish**.
Each has long, stiff, sharp spines
on its fins.
Each spine holds a powerful venom.
The fish use their spines to protect
themselves.

The small, pretty **blue-ringed octopus**
lives in the waters around Australia.
People often pick this octopus up
for a closer look.
SNAP!
The octopus bites.
Its deadly venom kills some people.

A jellyfish is a sea animal that looks like a blob of jelly.
But lots of long strings hang down from its body.
And each string has lots of stingers.

Sometimes a fish touches one of the jellyfish's strings.
The string shoots out short, sharp threads covered with venom.
Some hit the fish.
Soon the fish cannot move.
The jellyfish slowly pulls the fish up into its mouth.

The most venomous jellyfish is
the sea wasp.
It looks like half a soccer ball floating
in the water.
Hanging down from its body are
about 60 strings.
Each one is as long as
a telephone pole.

Swimmers in the waters
off Australia watch out
for sea wasps.
Their venom is strong
enough to kill
a person!

Lots of animals — from bees to ants, spiders to snakes, lizards to jellyfish — are dangerous creatures.
Some use their venom or poison to defend themselves.
Others use it to hunt prey.
But all of these animals need venom or poison to live.
Without it, none of them would be able to survive in the wild.